What are you going to do with that Booger?

by Roxy Humphrey

Illustrated by Marina Saumell

Published by Roxy Humphrey
Printed in the United States of America

Illustrated by Marina Saumell

ISBN: 9780578771830

This book is dedicated to
all those who teach the youngest learners
in our world.

It was a school day.
All of the children were gathered around the teacher.

It was story time.
The children loved listening to a good story.

Today:

The Tale
of Peter Rabbit

The teacher noticed a little child
sitting near the side of the group.
He was playing with something sticky.

All of the students heard their teacher ask,

"So, what are you going to do
with that booger?"

"Can I **keep** it?" asked Mason.

"**No,**" said the children.

"No," replied the teacher smiling.

"Can I **hide** it?" asked Mason.

"**No,**" said the children.

"**No,**" calmly replied the teacher.

"Can I **share** it?" asked Mason.

"No," said the children.

"No," replied the teacher using a firm voice.

"Can I **play** with it?" asked Mason.

"Can I **eat** it?" asked Mason.

"No!"

shouted the children.

"No,"

replied the teacher
in a louder voice.

Once again, the students heard
the teacher ask the child,

"So, what are you going to do
with that booger?"

Mason looked at his friends
and then at his teacher.
After thinking really hard, he asked,

"Can I **put it in a tissue
and throw it away?"**

"Yes!" shouted all the children and the teacher together.

Everyone had smiles on their faces,
with their teacher having the biggest smile of all.

THE END

About the Author

Roxy Humphrey lives in Minnesota, and yes, enjoys the snow in the winter as much as boating on the rivers and beautiful lakes during the summer months. She currently is a fifth grade teacher and has been awarded the Walmart local "Teacher of the Year". Roxy's also received the "Cooperating Teacher in Elementary Education" award from the University of Wisconsin-River Falls.

She has five kids of her own and two grandchildren. Roxy currently has on her hobby farm chickens, bunnies, two dogs, several flower and vegetable gardens, and one loving husband who is her greatest supporter and friend.

CPSIA information can be obtained
at www.ICGtesting.com
Printed in the USA
BVHW020816130421
604812BV00003B/85